Kamala H

MW01140142

CHERRY LAKE PRESS

Published in the United States of America by Cherry Lake Publishing Group
Ann Arbor, Michigan
www.cherrylakepublishing.com

Reading Adviser: Beth Walker Gambro, MS, Ed., Reading Consultant, Yorkville, IL
Book Designer: Jennifer Wahi
Illustrator: Jeff Bane

Photo Credits: ©Photo by Jim Heaphy/Uploaded by Cullen328/Wikimedia, 5; ©Ink Drop/Shutterstock, 7; ©wonderlustpicstravel/Shutterstock, 9; ©lev radin/Shutterstock, 11; © Neon Tommy/Photo by Shotgun Spratling/flickr, 13; © Andreistanescu/Dreamstime, 15; ©Office of the Attorney General of California/Wikimedia, 17; ©Stratos Brilakis/Shutterstock, 19; ©BiksuTong/Shutterstock, 21; Cover, 1, 6, 10, 14, 18, Jeff Bane; Various frames throughout, Shutterstock

Copyright ©2022 by Cherry Lake Publishing Group
All rights reserved. No part of this book may be reproduced or utilized in any form or by any means without written permission from the publisher.

Cherry Lake Press is an imprint of Cherry Lake Publishing Group.

Library of Congress Cataloging-in-Publication Data

Names: Sarantou, Katlin, author. | Bane, Jeff, 1957- illustrator.
Title: Kamala Harris / Katlin Sarantou ; illustrated by Jeff Bane.
Description: Ann Arbor, Michigan : Cherry Lake Publishing, 2021. | Series:
   My itty-bitty bio | Includes index.
Identifiers: LCCN 2021007977 (print) | LCCN 2021007978 (ebook) | ISBN
   9781534186910 (hardcover) | ISBN 9781534188310 (paperback) | ISBN
   9781534189713 (pdf) | ISBN 9781534191112 (ebook)
Subjects: LCSH: Harris, Kamala, 1964---Juvenile literature. |
   Vice-presidents--United States--Biography--Juvenile literature. | Women
   legislators--United States--Biography--Juvenile literature. | African
   American women legislators--Biography--Juvenile literature.
Classification: LCC E901.1.H37 S27 2021 (print) | LCC E901.1.H37 (ebook)
   | DDC 973.934092 [B]--dc23
LC record available at https://lccn.loc.gov/2021007977
LC ebook record available at https://lccn.loc.gov/2021007978

Printed in the United States of America
Corporate Graphics

About the author: Katlin Sarantou grew up in the cornfields of Ohio. She enjoys reading and dreaming of faraway places.

About the illustrator: Jeff Bane and his two business partners own a studio along the American River in Folsom, California, home of the 1849 Gold Rush. When Jeff's not sketching or illustrating for clients, he's either swimming or kayaking in the river to relax.

My name is Kamala Harris.

I was born in California. The year was 1964.

My parents are **immigrants**.

My mother came from India.
My father came from Jamaica.

I went to a mostly White school as a child.

I was part of a **desegregation** program.

I was inspired by civil rights leaders. I went to law school.

Who inspires you?

I became **District Attorney** of San Francisco in California.

I was later elected California's **Attorney General**.

I was then elected to the U.S. **Senate**.

I help carve a path for others.

I fight for the rights of people. I fight to raise **wages**. I fight to make **health care** more available.

What would you fight for?

Joe Biden ran for United States president in 2020. He asked me to join him.

On January 20, 2021, I became U.S. vice president. I am proud to be the first woman in this job. It's taken 231 years.

What would you like to ask me?

2016

1960

Born
1964

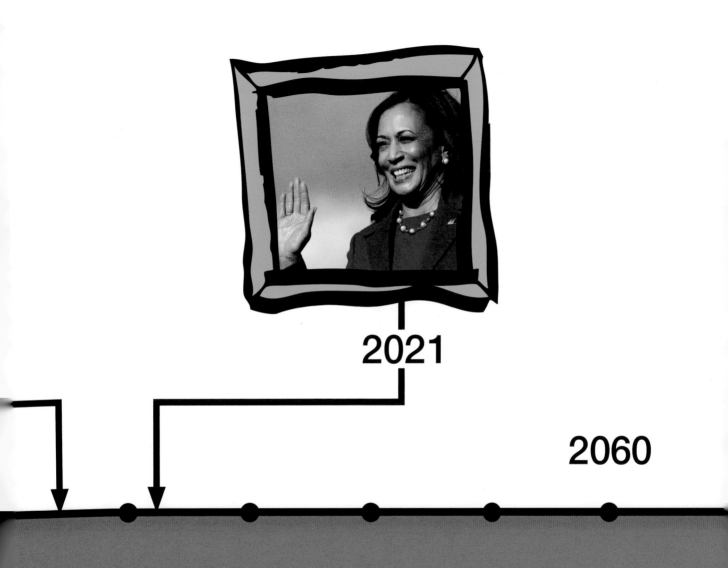

2021

2060

glossary

Attorney General (uh-TUR-nee JEN-ur-uhl) a person who represents a state in legal matters

desegregation (dee-seg-ruh-GAY-shuhn) the act of ending the practice of keeping different races separate

District Attorney (DISS-trikt uh-TUR-nee) a public official who acts as a prosecutor for the state in court

health care (HELTH KAIR) access to doctors and medicine

immigrants (IM-uh-gruhnts) people who come from one country to live in another country

Senate (SEN-it) a governing body of the United States that votes on new laws

wages (WAJE-ez) the money you make from working

index